GREAT AMERICAN BUILDINGS

Origami cutouts of everybody's favorite landmarks

ORIGAMI ARCHITECTURE by
Masahiro Chatani and
Keiko Nakazawa

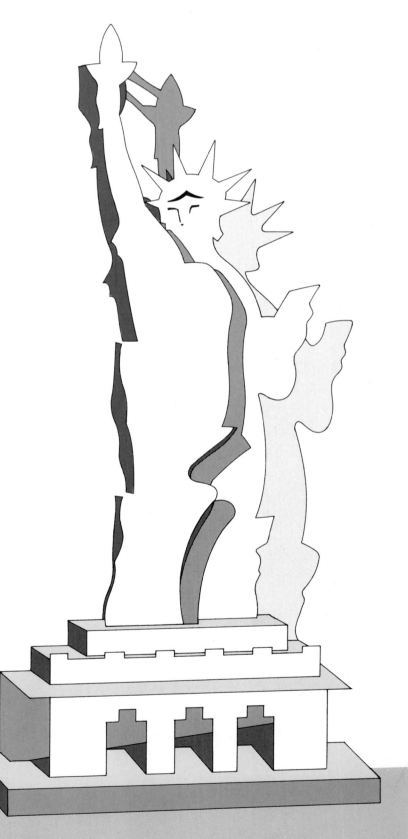

KODANSHA INTERNATIONAL
Tokyo • New York • London

Patterns 3-5, 8-21, 23, and 25 designed by Masahiro Chatani
Patterns 1, 2, 6, 7, 22, and 24 designed by Keiko Nakazawa
Schematics by Yasunori Yoshida
Translation by Mark Oshima

Distributed in the United States by Kodansha America, Inc., 114
Fifth Avenue, New York, N.Y., 10011, and in the United Kingdom
and continental Europe by Kodansha Europe Ltd., Gillingham
House, 38-44, Gillingham Street, London SW1V 1HU. Published
by Kodansha International Ltd., 17-14, Otowa 1-chome, Bunkyo-ku,
Tokyo 112, and Kodansha America, Inc.

91 92 93 10 9 8 7 6 5 4 3 2 1

Library of Congress Cataloging-in-Publication Data
Chatani, Masahiro.
Great American Buildings: origami cutouts of everybody's favorite
   landmarks: origami architecture / by Masahiro Chatani and Keiko
   Nakazawa; translated by Mark Oshima; photographs by Akihiko
   Tokue.—1st ed.

   1. Origami.   2. Architectural models—United States.
   3. Buildings—United States.   I. Nakazawa, Keiko.   II. Titles.
TT870.C457 1991   736'962—dc20   91-6463

ISBN 4-7700-1538-0

Contents

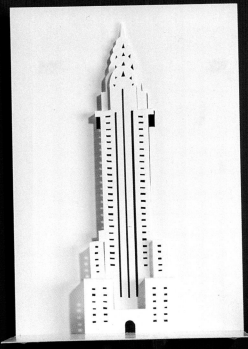

2. Chrysler Building

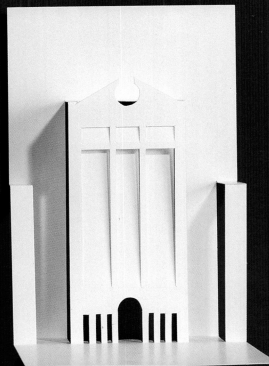

1. Empire State Building

3. AT&T Building

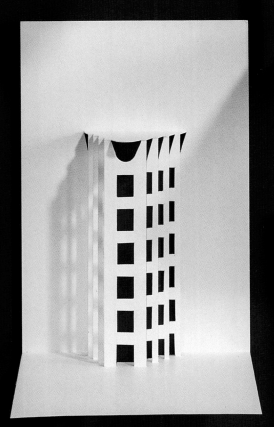

5. Flatiron Building

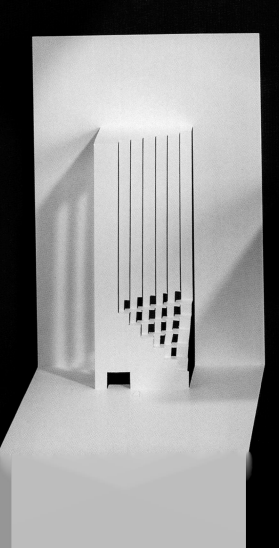

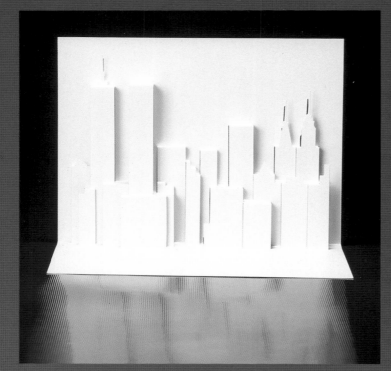

7. Manhattan Skyline

8. Guggenheim Museum

9. Museum of Modern Art

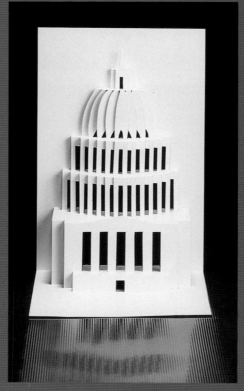

10. Capitol Building

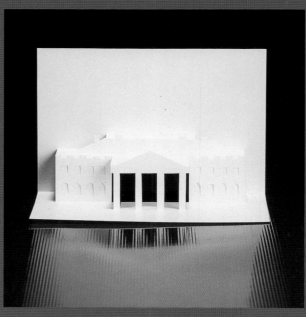

11. White House (*front*)

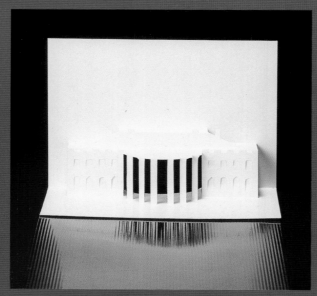

12. White House (*back*)

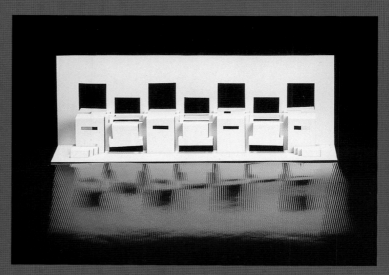

13. National Air & Space Museum

14. Dulles International Airport

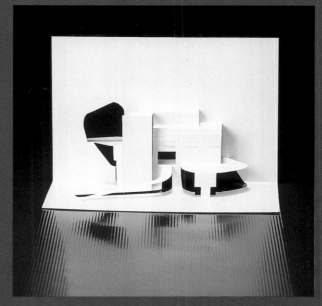

15. Carpenter Center
(Harvard University)

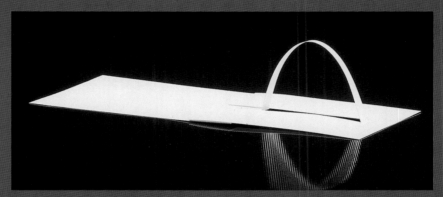

16. Gateway Arch

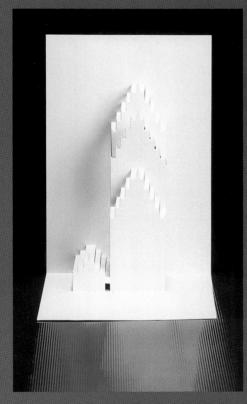

17. Republic Bank Center

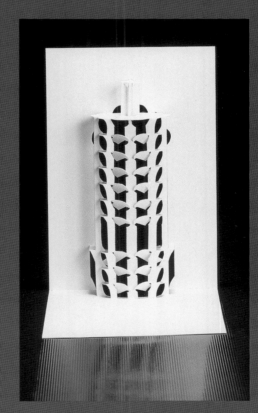

18. Marina City

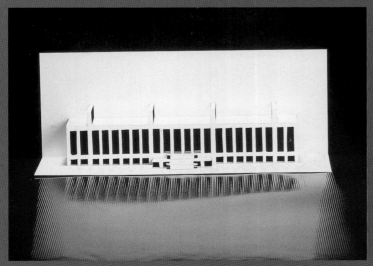

19. Crown Hall (Illinois Institute of Technology)

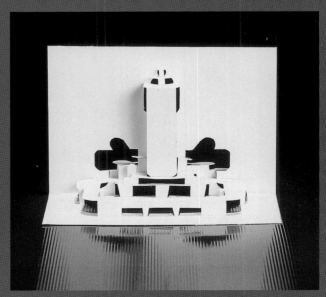

20. Johnson Wax Buildings

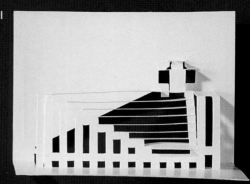

21. Hyatt Regency Hotel

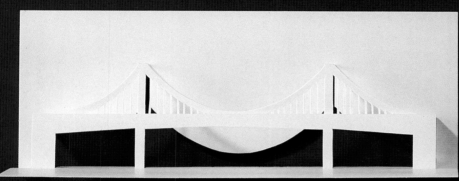

22. Golden Gate Bridge

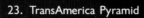

23. TransAmerica Pyramid

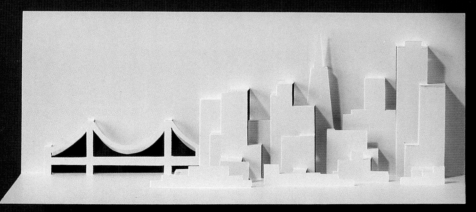

24. San Francisco Skyline

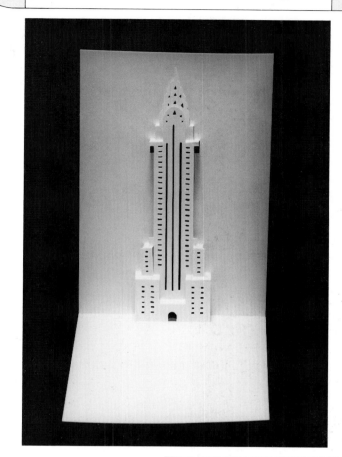

1929–31

Richmond H. Shreve (1877-1946)
William F. Lamb (1883-1952)
Arthur L. Harmon (1876-1958)

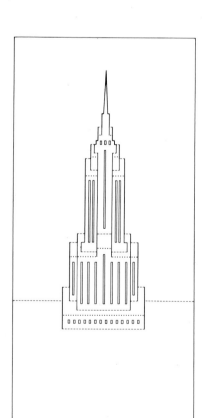

Even today, sightseers stream to the Empire State Building for the magnificent view from its observation platform. For forty-two years, until the World Trade Center was built in 1973, it was the tallest building in the world.

Construction began in a time of prosperity, and due to advanced construction methods, it took only eighteen months to complete. But when the building opened its doors, America was in the depths of the Depression. Fear about the state of the economy resulted in vast stretches of unlet office space, earning it the nickname "the Empty State Building" for a time.

There are a total of sixty-seven elevators in the core of the building. On the 102nd floor, there is a tower with a mast 197 feet tall for a total height of 1,250 feet. The mast was originally intended as a mooring for zeppelins.

By 1952, a 222-foot television tower had been added, making the world's tallest building even taller: 1,472 feet.

First, carefully cut out the small windows and long, thin rectangles. This building is composed entirely of right angles and there is not much space between the windows, so be sure to mark all lines firmly and accurately with your stylus and to mark and cut out the lines with precision. Be especially careful with the horizontal mountain and valley folds, because if they are not perfectly parallel, the completed building will lean to one side. Be sure to do a nice job of cutting out the pointed top of the building.

1928–30

William Van Alen (1883-1954)

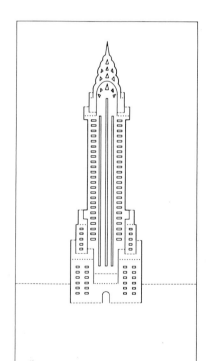

New York's unofficial race to build the world's tallest building began in 1908 with the 612-foot Singer Tower. This was soon followed by the 700-foot Metropolitan Life Insurance Tower in 1909 and then the Woolworth Building (1913), which, at 792 feet, held the title until 1931, when it was surpassed by the Empire State Building.

William Van Alen's original plan for the Chrysler Building would have made it 925 feet tall, but in 1929, Van Alen heard that his former partner, H. Craig Severance, and Severance's new partner, Yasuo Matsui, were planning the main building of the Bank of Manhattan Company. This was to be 927 feet tall. Van Alen immediately worked out a plan to construct a spire on top of his building, for a total height of 1,048 feet, making it the tallest in the world. He kept his addition secret until the building was completed in 1930, only to lose out to the Empire State Building soon after.

The Art Deco design for the spire is said to have been copied from the hood ornament of the company president's car. Its stainless-steel fans are truly impressive and somehow symbolic of the American dream.

First, be sure that the parallel mountain and valley folds are scored accurately. When you begin cutting, start with the windows and then work on the spire. Just fold slowly, with even and controlled pressure, to keep the main face of the building from bending because of the many windows.

1979–84

Philip Johnson (1906-   )
John Burgee (1933-   )
See also no. 17.

Before becoming an architect, Philip Johnson was a director of New York's Museum of Modern Art (*see no. 9*) and an architecture critic. Though his first work, the Glass House, was not designed until 1949, he is today one of the oldest active architects in the world, and continues to outperform many of his younger colleagues.

The design of the broken pediment on the top of the building was inspired by the work of Thomas Chippendale (1718-79), who is remembered today mostly for his ornamental furniture designs. The AT&T Building was Johnson's first work to directly incorporate past styles. Though controversial when it was first unveiled, it is a prime example of the architectural movement from pure functionalism to expressive decoration.

At 647 feet and 37 stories, the main headquarters of one of the largest and most powerful companies in the world makes its statement with robust majesty.

When cutting, be sure that the long straight lines are true. After the cutting is finished, begin putting creases in the long folds, because these are the most difficult, and work your way down to the short folds. Push the windows inside a bit so that they are diagonal to help give the right feeling.

1983

Der Scutt (1934-   )

Trump Tower sits on Fifth Avenue, affording its famous owner, Donald Trump, an expansive view of Manhattan. Its glittering curtain of glass extends fifty-four stories, the stepped lower half serving as the atrium roof. During the day there is the lush greenery of "the roof-top garden," and at night the twinkling lights remind one of a Christmas tree. There may be petty gossip about Donald Trump, but by contrast, the building itself, built on a grand scale, sparkles. Upon entering the lobby and stepping onto the escalator, one is immediately overwhelmed by the atrium lined with gold mirrors. Though the lavishness is at times unsettling, the tower seems the most sympathetic architectural rendering of New York today.

The part of the building with the staggered layers is difficult, so be careful to cut this out precisely. If you make a mistake, fix it from the back of the paper right away. If you don't, the mistake will get bigger and the other cuts will be thrown off as well. When folding, gently do the center valley fold first and the main horizontal fold second, as usual, but next, instead of folding the short horizontal folds along the top and the base, begin gently pulling up the mountain folds in the staggered-layer area. When the layers begin to take shape, make the short horizontal folds along the top and the base.

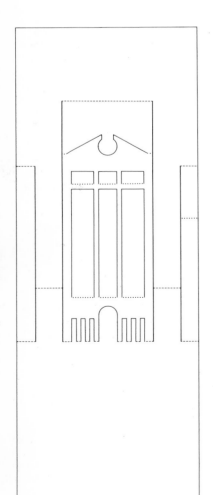

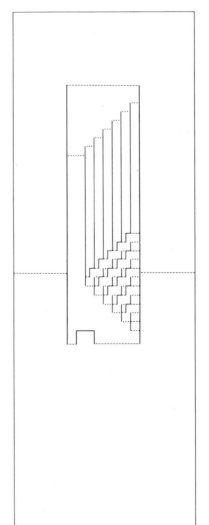

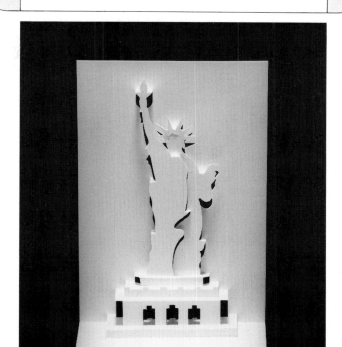

1901–03
Originally the Fuller Building

Daniel H. Burnham (1846–1912)

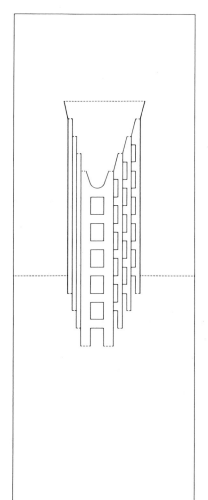

New York's first period of high-rise buildings began in 1903. This building was erected on a triangular site facing Madison Square where Fifth Avenue meets Broadway. At 283 feet, it is not particularly tall, but its sharp, erect, triangular form is a fine example of using an oddly shaped lot to good advantage. The traditional three-tier construction taken from the Italian Renaissance displays wonderful variety and rhythm, but at the time it was built it was severely criticized by New Yorkers, perhaps because the architect was a member of the Chicago school, which relied on a rich variety of decorative resources. At present, for some reason, the exterior walls have been covered with a postmodern surface, but I hope that someday the original monumental surface will be restored.

When he designed this building, the architect, Daniel H. Burnham, was already known for a number of buildings in Chicago, including the Rookery Building (1884–86) and the Reliance Building (1894), but these were achievements accomplished with his partner, John Wellborn Root (1850–91). With the Flatiron Building, Burnham confirmed his reputation as an architect of talent.

This model has been designed simply in order to give the feeling of a triangular building. The long, narrow strips from the base to the top are delicate, so be careful not to bend them when folding; otherwise, this is an easy card to make.

1886

Frédéric Bartholdi (1834–1904)
sculptor
Alexandre Eiffel (1832–1923)
engineer

The French government sent this monument to the United States government in 1886, on the occasion of the hundredth anniversary of the Declaration of Independence, as a sign of friendship between the people of the two countries.

Frédéric Bartholdi, who showed a particular flair for monumental sculpture, began hammering out the 3/32-inch-thick copper plates to form the 151-foot creation in 1877. In 1881 he asked Alexandre Eiffel to plan a framework to support the statue. An experienced designer of bridges, Eiffel constructed an iron truss tower capable of withstanding high winds. In 1884 the statue was completed and then the process of dismantling it and sending it to America began. (In the same year, Eiffel brought forth his plan for the 985-foot Eiffel Tower.)

This figure of a goddess holding a flaming torch high in her right hand stands 302 feet tall, with pedestal; in her left hand is the Declaration of Independence. She was the first thing to greet the shiploads of people emigrating from Europe—a truly overwhelming sight.

Since the figure of the Statue of Liberty is full of curves, the challenge is to see how flowingly you can cut the lines. Be careful in cutting out the spikes of the crown. Cut the curves in a comfortable direction, moving both the paper and the blade. Be precise when folding, and pay attention to the base of the statue. Since the horizontal mountain fold is rather long, the half-cut should be deep.

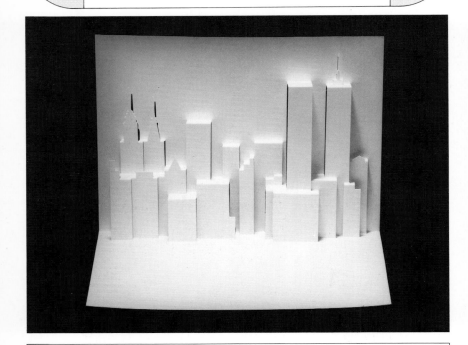

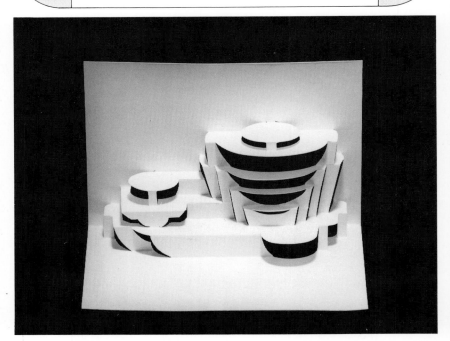

View from the New Jersey side of the Hudson River

Manhattan: a center of politics, fashion, and culture. Of all the beautiful views of New York—from the Queensborough Bridge at night, from the Brooklyn Bridge, from across a Brooklyn cemetery, from a helicopter, from Liberty Island—this is my favorite. The skyline sparkling in the light of the setting sun is absolutely breathtaking.

The twin towers on the right side of the skyline in the card compose the 110-story World Trade Center, designed by Minoru Yamasaki (1912–86). The tower with the antenna has an observation deck open to the public; the other tower has a helicopter pad on the roof. The tall buildings on the left side are the Empire State Building (no. 1) and the Chrysler Building (no. 2).

Compositions that use up an entire big sheet of paper have an outsized pleasure all their own. The raised and recessed portions look difficult, but just fold them carefully, little by little, applying light pressure to the entire card. Your fingers may not reach the center, but if you crease each fold first and then fold the whole card, it may be easier. Take your time and rest frequently; don't rush. Just like Rome, New York wasn't built in a day. Try some variations if you like. You can cut out windows, using the cover of this book as a guide, and you can add your favorite buildings to make your own New York.

Oblivious to the urban landscape around it, the Guggenheim is more of a museum piece than a museum. Although Wright began designing the Guggenheim in 1943, he did not settle on the final design until 1951. Construction was completed in 1959, the year of Wright's death, so he never lived to hear the great volume of praise and criticism this work provoked.

As in most of Wright's buildings, the entrance is understated, but it suddenly opens out on a spacious atrium ninety-two feet high. Visitors go up a small elevator to the top of the building and then view the exhibition as they walk down a spiral ramp. A daring plan. More people stop to gaze at the atrium than to look at the exhibits. In fact, it is said that the slanting ramp actually makes the paintings look unbalanced. This dramatic yet incongruous building may have been more at home in the Arizona desert, where we can find other Wright masterpieces, and its idiosyncracies present special challenges for the curator.

How cleanly you can cut out the circular cone will show your true skill. But the real building is rather rough in form, so that even if you waver a bit, this is likely to add to the charm of the card. Remember to move the paper and the cutter in opposite directions when cutting curves, but keep the blade away from your fingers. For the long horizontal fold, half-cut accurately and then fold carefully.

I understand that a sleek and straight, decidedly un-Wrightian high-rise addition is now under construction on the left side of the museum. If you want a challenge, you can add this part to the card yourself.

1956–59

Frank L. Wright
(1867–1959)
See also no. 20.

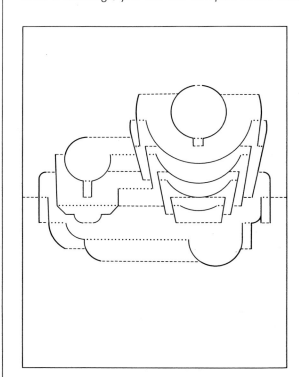

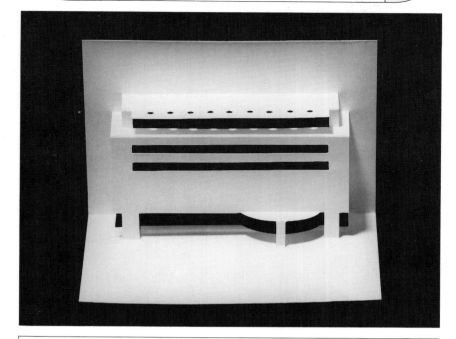

The Museum of Modern Art is a classic example of the orthodox international style in its early stages. Along with its contents, the building itself has become a mecca of modern design not only for America but for the world.

Edward Durrell Stone designed this austere building under the guidance of Phillip Goodwin, and it was this work that made his reputation. After its completion, he set up an independent office and moved toward a more ornamental style. The American Embassy in New Delhi, India (1954), is representative of his new style, but the Museum of Modern Art is his most successful work. The 1951 addition was one of Philip Johnson's first designs. He also contributed a notable garden in 1964. (*For other examples of Johnson's work, see nos. 3 and 17.*)

The round holes are the only difficult part of this card. If you use a punch for leather work or a paper punch that makes the right-size holes, even this difficulty will be eliminated. The half-cut for the mountain fold that forms the top of the building should be rather deep or the card will be hard to fold.

Using this design as a base, try taking a large sheet of paper and designing your own additions: the expansions on either side and the new entrance are some variations you can attempt.

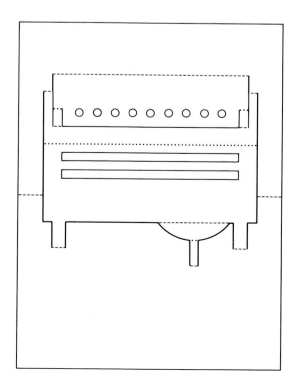

1939

Edward D. Stone
(1902-78)
Phillip L. Goodwin
(1885-1958)

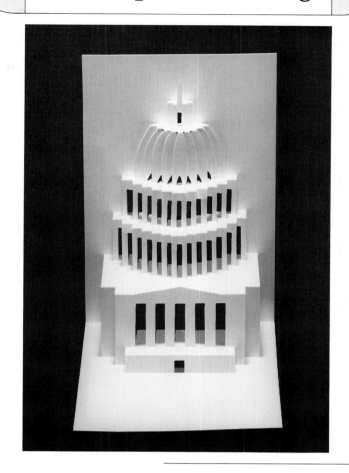

1773–1862

William Thornton (1759-1828)
Benjamin H. Latrobe (1764-1820)
Charles Bulfinch (1763-1844)
Robert Mills (1781-1855)
Thomas U. Walter (1804-88)

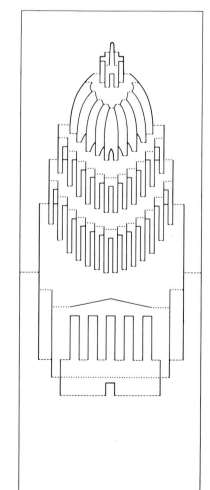

It required four separate periods of building before this symbol of America was complete. In the first competition to design the Capitol in 1791, there were no winning entries, but several months later an amateur architect named William Thornton, an Englishman who had just moved from the West Indies, won the competition with a design featuring a dome styled after the Pantheon in Rome.

Because Thornton was not a professional architect, the actual construction plans were entrusted to the French architect Étienne Sulpice Hallet (1755-1825), who had placed second in the competition. Unfortunately, Hallet tried to modify the plan to resemble his own, so in 1794 he was dismissed.

In 1814 the building was burned by the British army, but was soon rebuilt. Later, due to a request from Congress, the central dome was expanded to its present height (222 feet) and diameter (98 feet), giving it the graceful "wedding-cake" form that it has today.

The challenge of this design is in expressing the shape of the dome. Moreover, the symmetrical design requires even more care and effort than usual, since the two sides have to look alike. Remember to start cutting from the small cuts and start folding from the large folds. Once you've started folding the center valley, pull up on the spire of the building and make creases in the folds around it. Then the building will take shape naturally.

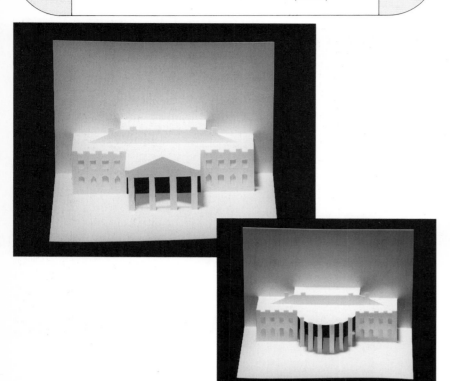

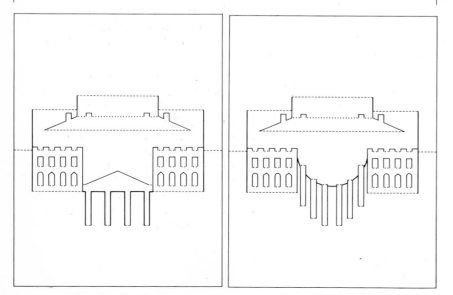

James Hoban, a famous Irish-born architect, won the competition to design the executive mansion with a Palladian-style design. President Washington selected the site himself, but died before the building was completed.

The porticoes on both sides, north and south, were added in 1807 by the English architect Benjamin Latrobe (*see also no. 10*). The upper parts of the windows on the first floor and the railing on the roof are based on European palace style, with alternating arches and triangles.

In the summer of 1814 the British army torched the executive mansion along with the Capitol Building; then, like an act of divine providence, a hurricane inflicted severe damage on the British army.

After the fire, the stone outer walls were painted white to conceal the damage. Since 1818 the building has been called the White House and it has been painted white ever since.

FOR BOTH VIEWS

Be clean and careful when you cut out the windows. Before you start folding, push them in slightly to make sure they're cut correctly. If the valley fold across the top of the roof is scored well, the building will be easy to fold. If you have difficulty folding it, try making a half-cut on the reverse side along this valley fold. Both cards are simple designs that can be attempted by beginners.

It may be fun to add the gardens to both sides and then to put the two cards together back-to-back.

1793–1829

James Hoban (c. 1762–1829) Benjamin H. Latrobe (1764–1820)

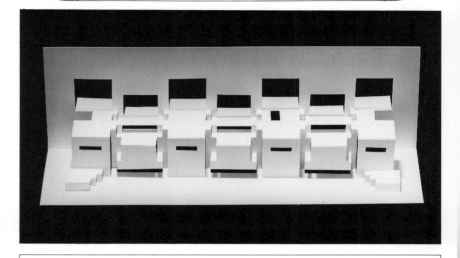

Along the grassy mall that runs between the Capitol Building and the Washington Monument there is a series of museums and art galleries with exhibition space devoted to the cultures and civilizations of the world, all of them falling under the auspices of the Smithsonian Institution. The National Air & Space Museum is one of the newest and most popular of these buildings, containing exhibits ranging from the Wright Brothers' first plane to space rockets.

This museum was very long in coming . . . *thirty years* from idea to reality. The law authorizing the project was enacted in 1946, but it was not until 1958 that the site was decided upon—and another six years went by before Hellmuth, Obata & Kassabaum (HOK) was selected in 1964. HOK proceeded to complete the design on schedule and within the budget, only to see the project put on hold for the next six years due to the nation's fiscal complications brought on by the Vietnam War. Resurrected in 1970, the project survived six more years of ups and downs and was ultimately completed precisely on time to take its place as one of the major participating institutions in the 1976 bicentennial celebration.

The building's design has a history of its own. Officially, the design finally succeeded on the third try, but in fact it had succeeded on the *first* try; the initial design had to be abandoned only because the government—having delayed the project for six years—still wanted to build it at the original 1964 prices in spite of 1970's significantly escalated construction costs. The second try, starting from scratch, was successful in the eyes of all of the relevant governing committees except one: the Fine Arts Commission eventually rejected the design. The third design, again from scratch, is what we see and enjoy today.

Since this card is very wide, be especially careful in folding across the width. It may be easier if you half-cut the long valley folds from the back. Take your time and fold carefully, starting with the center valley fold, then the long horizontal mountain folds. Pull the short mountain folds toward you with your tweezers.

1976

George F. Hellmuth (1907-) Gyo Obata (1923-), **principal designer**
George E. Kassabaum (1920-82)

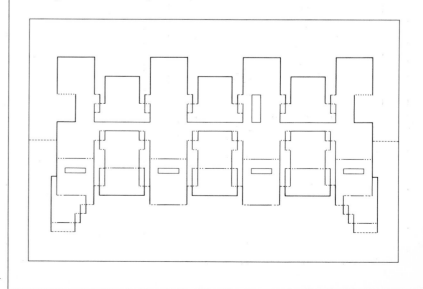

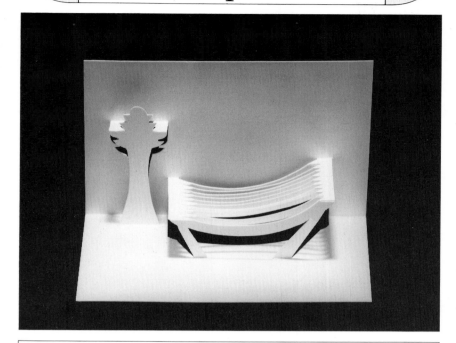

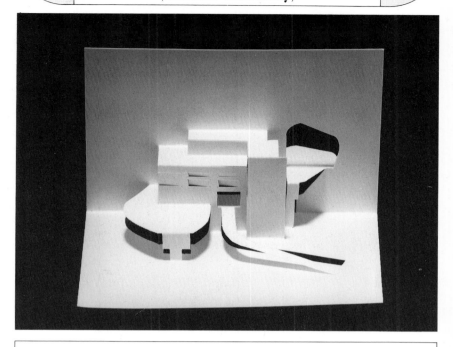

This daring design with its suspended roof that looks almost airborne is the ultimate expression of airport architecture. Dulles Airport was originally equipped with special buses called Mobile Lounges that took passengers from the terminal to the airplane. This revolutionary system allowed the building itself to be very simple. Dulles Airport was built just as long-distance travel was making the transition from propellers to jet engines, requiring new airport architecture.

The designer, Eero Saarinen, also constructed the TWA terminal at Kennedy Airport in New York at about the same time. That building is reminiscent of an enormous bird in flight. Both structures are masterpieces that cannot fail to capture the imagination of travelers.

Now that jumbo jets are commonplace and security measures have grown strict, passengers at Dulles board their planes along extendable ramps, as they would at any other airport. Fortunately, this additional work was accomplished without impairing the intent of the original design.

The many curves in this design may make the card a bit confusing to fold, but if you pull out the mountain folds to the left and right of the arch first, and follow the standard order for the rest, everything will go smoothly. After you finish folding, use your fingers to push out the roof into the inverted arch that will complete the card.

1958–62
Eero Saarinen
(1910–61)
See also no. 16.

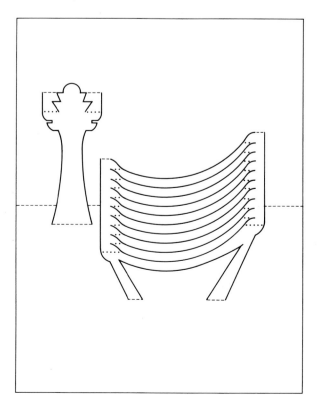

Carpenter Center does not particularly stand out in the extensive campus of Harvard, yet in the world of design it is famous for being the only American building designed by Le Corbusier.

Le Corbusier was always concerned with the relationship between a building and the city surrounding it. Carpenter Center is practically a museum of Le Corbusier design—a compendium of the trademark features that made him famous in his youth—and an attractive one at that. The building is raised on pillars; this "pilotis" structure allows the spaces inside and outside the building to blend freely. The ramp passing through the middle of the building is almost an extension of the sidewalk, and the "brise soleil" window slats filter natural light through the rooms.

Born in Switzerland, Le Corbusier produced one new idea after another from his workshop in Paris, and it was his work there that began to influence architects around the world. Eventually he completed several famous compositions which established his place in architectural history.

This card's subtle curves and complex folds may be a bit difficult, but these are the features that give this design its character. The construction of the ramp is intriguing—it gets tucked away neatly when the card is folded, but when the card is opened it pops out just right! The actual folding is not that difficult, so work slowly and carefully, constantly referring to the photograph of the completed card.

1961–63
Le Corbusier
(1887-1965)

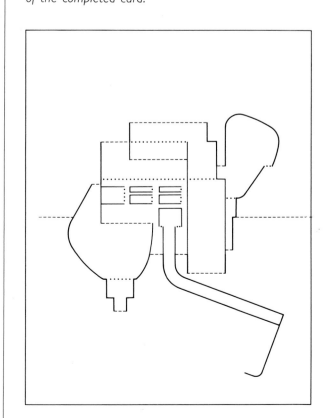

16 ST. LOUIS
Gateway Arch
Level C

17 HOUSTON
Republic Bank Center
Level B

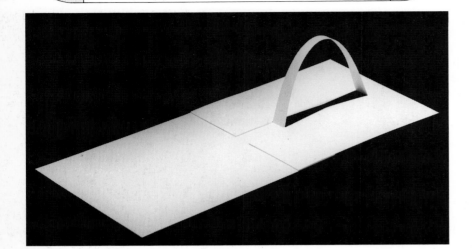

To commemorate Thomas Jefferson's 1803 acquisition of French territory west of the Mississippi River (the Louisiana Purchase), the stretches of warehouses on the west bank of the river were transformed into a beautiful park in 1935. Twelve years later architect Eero Saarinen won a design competition with a spectacular plan for a monument to the westward expansion. Saarinen's arch symbolized the achievement in what he called a simple but impressive form comparable to an obelisk or a pyramid.

Six hundred and thirty feet tall (with the distance between the base pillars being 630 feet as well), this arch is built in the form of a catenary, which is the curve made by a piece of string held at both ends. The shape is elegant and natural and the arch's stainless-steel surface is breathtaking, reflecting the light of the sun during the day and the moon at night. The idea of providing transportation to the top of the arch from an underground space via small linked capsules is also brilliant. The views to the east and west from the top of the arch are indescribably wonderful.

Born in Finland, Saarinen was the son of Eliel Gottlieb Saarinen, architect of Helsinki Station (completed in 1914), and often thought of as the father of modern architecture in Finland. In 1922 the father won second place in a design competition for the Chicago Tribune Building and moved to the United States to take advantage of the wealth of jobs. Eero was then thirteen.

The St. Louis Gateway was Eero's first work after becoming independent of his father's firm. After that, the young Saarinen took off like a ship in full sail and displayed a true flair for design. Dulles International Airport (no. 14) is a prime example of the new and individualistic directions his work began to take. Unfortunately, he died only eleven years after his father. If he were alive today he would be in his eighties and without a doubt would be considered, along with Mies, Wright, and Le Corbusier, a master of modern architecture.

This arch comes jumping out from one sheet of paper. The overlapping portions must be glued together, making this card different from the others.

Cut carefully so that the curve will take an elegant shape. Holding all your fingers together, bend slowly. The beauty of the curve of the arch will be an indication of your abilities, so re-create it with this in mind.

1962–68

Eero Saarinen (1910–61)
See also no. 14.

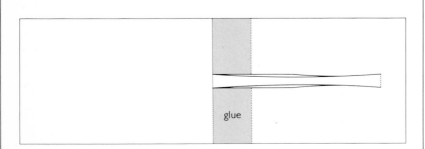

glue

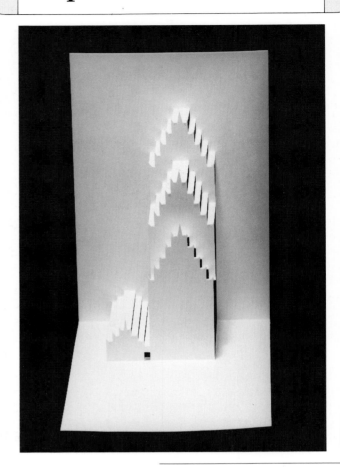

1981–84

Philip Johnson (1906–   )
John Burgee (1933–   )
See also no. 3.

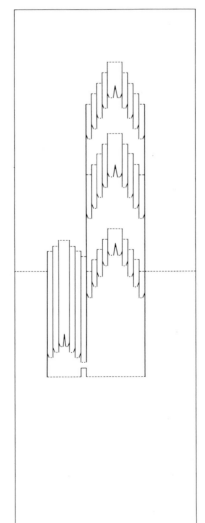

By the end of 1980, the prosperity brought by increased oil production, the space industry, and new high-tech companies had utterly transformed the skyline of Houston and its surroundings. In the midst of a group of tall buildings (the highest being 75 stories and 1,000 feet tall), the Republic Bank Center faces the expanse of Jones Plaza with a calm and classical facade. Seven hundred and eighty feet in height, with 56 stories, it has been left far behind in the race to be the tallest building, but it has a glorious design that sets it far ahead of the others.

The rust-colored stone facing is striking for its modernity, but the gabled three-step roof creates the atmosphere of a Gothic cathedral. On the cut-out steps of the roof, little obelisk-shaped pillars give the building an elegant air.

This building is clearly distinguished from the glass boxes and concrete structures that surround it. It looks as if it might have been standing there for over a century, and simultaneously as if it is a visitor from a future civilization. Its timelessness is truly remarkable.

The most difficult part of this design is cutting out the small obelisks on each level. Be careful about the long straight cuts as well, and the tiny horizontal pieces that hold the card together are very delicate. But these details are the life of this particular design, and of the building itself.

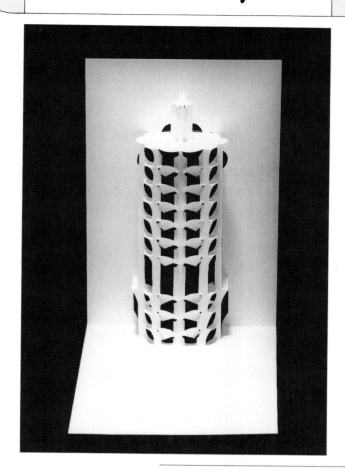

The main floor of Crown Hall is composed entirely of a huge universal space 120 by 220 feet with an 18-foot ceiling supported by large beams and no pillars. Small individual rooms and lavatories are hidden half underground. This open, glass-walled structure is in the stoic Bauhaus style of all the buildings on the IIT campus, but is also its culminating work, and in its austerity serves to exemplify the rest of the campus.

When Ludwig Mies left Berlin in 1938, fleeing Nazi persecution, he moved to Chicago and became the main architecture instructor at IIT. In 1939 he produced the overall plan for the entire IIT campus, making ample use of the "infinite space" design that Crown Hall displays so well. Construction began in 1943 and Crown Hall was the final building to be completed.

In Berlin, Mies had worked in the office of Peter Behrens (1868–1940), who can be called the father of modern architecture. There he worked together with such future giants of modern architecture as Walter Gropius (1883–1969) and Le Corbusier (*see no. 15*). In 1919, Mies paved the way for modern architecture with a design for a twenty-story office building completely covered with glass curtain walls. Later, his unflagging pursuit of simple designs based on steel-frame construction influenced architects the world over and became known as the "Miesian" style. New York's Seagram Building, completely clothed in bronze-colored outer walls, is widely regarded as Mies's masterpiece.

Mies's buildings are among those with the simplest construction but expressing the deepest beauty.

The cutting and folding are not particularly difficult, but since you must repeat very fine movements, please be patient as you complete this design. The front steps are wide but not high, so make the half-cuts rather deep, and pay attention to the mountain fold across the top of the building. When folding, go slowly so that the four long bars on the roof do not bend at the point where they meet the main horizontal mountain fold.

1955–56

Ludwig Mies Van der Rohe (1886–1969)

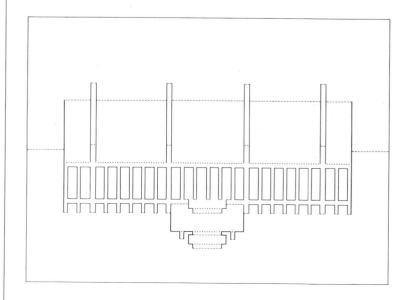

1960–62

Bertrand Goldberg (1913–   )

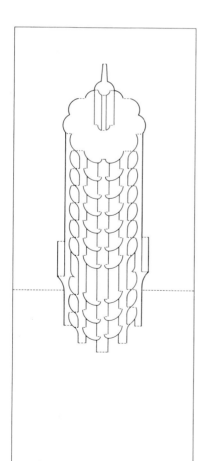

Marina City, built on the Chicago River, is made up of twin cylinders of reinforced concrete. When these towers were completed in 1962, they were the tallest reinforced-concrete structures in the world (684 feet high). Marina City is a fascinating structure, with berths for boats on the river, a spiral parking garage up to the nineteenth floor, and apartments up to the sixtieth floor. This type of architecture has gained the nickname of "corncob" architecture, because the curves of the balconies resemble those of kernels of corn, familiar yet elegant. This is the first downtown nursing home built in the United States. The sixteen-story business section at the rear boasts a movie theater and a shopping center, one of the first multi-use complexes in America. The cylindrical design is functional as well as attractive, and is completely filled by its elevators and staircases, so that one can see that this shape is practical and not just a whim of the architect.

Cut out the large and small curves carefully and take ample time to fold the card properly. When folding, pull up on the spire first, and then fold each of the balconies little by little. At first, the long pillars may bend a little, but they will slowly straighten out as you keep folding. The more pains you take, the happier you will be with the results when it is finished.

The Johnson Wax Buildings could have come from another time or another planet. The Research Tower, in contrast to the Administration Building, is a sturdy, square construction with rounded corners. It is clad in alternating bands of brick and glass tubing, through which one is offered a most stunning view of the night sky. However, like many of Frank Lloyd Wright's works, although the Research Tower succeeds aesthetically, its unique design proved to be impractical, and in this particular case the building had to be shut down.

After setting up an office independent of the famous Chicago architect Louis Sullivan (1856–1924), Wright turned his ambitions to his own unique organic expressions and completed numerous designs and masterpieces with great power. Wright studied the architectural decoration of the Mayan and Incan civilizations and separated himself from the influence of European styles very quickly to create a truly American architecture.

Remember to move the paper and the blade in opposite directions when cutting out the curves. Fold slowly, constantly referring to the photograph of the completed card. Begin with the center valley fold, then pull up the spire slightly. Next, proceed with the lower sections of the card: work from the periphery inward, folding the three center pillars last.

Wright's architecture contains the imprint of the whole history of architecture, and even hints at its future. If you come away with a better sense of Wright's style of design, then this origami architecture card will have been a success.

One of a series of Hyatt Hotel buildings, this San Francisco hotel on the Embarcadero has come to look quiet and settled, but inside, its dramatic atrium is world-class. The atrium soars over the spacious lobby and gradually narrows as it approaches the upper stories; it is like looking at the lofty spaces of a Gothic cathedral.

John Calvin Portman is the first of a new type of architect who is not merely an artist but an entrepreneur as well. Rather than waiting for clients to come to him, Portman generates his own proposals and takes them to potential clients. The success of the new four-star hotels that he has built all over America—in Chicago, Los Angeles, Detroit, and Atlanta—speaks for itself. Each of his hotels has an impressive and attractive exterior, with simple and frugal rooms that are a comfort to travelers.

Portman is pragmatic and very American; I have great hopes for his future creations.

Try to imagine the impact of the inner construction of this building by looking at the card from the back. Step by step, this structure creates a three- and four-dimensional drama of space.

Cut out the straight diagonal lines very carefully, and don't rush as you fold. Begin with the center valley fold and then work on the steps of the roof from the top down.

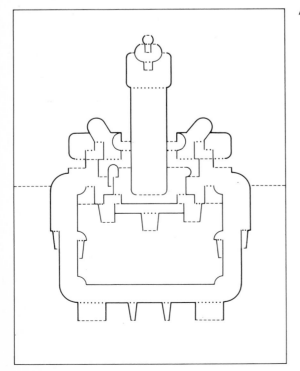

Administration Building:
1936–39
Research Tower:
1947–50

Frank L. Wright
(1867–1959)
See also no. 8.

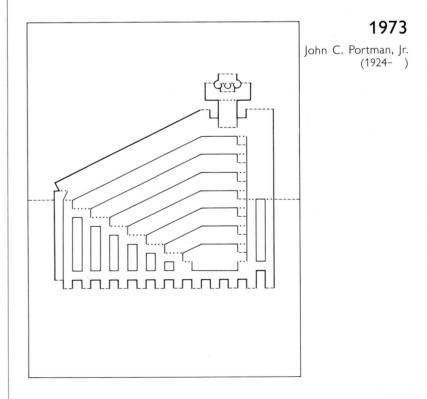

1973
John C. Portman, Jr.
(1924–   )

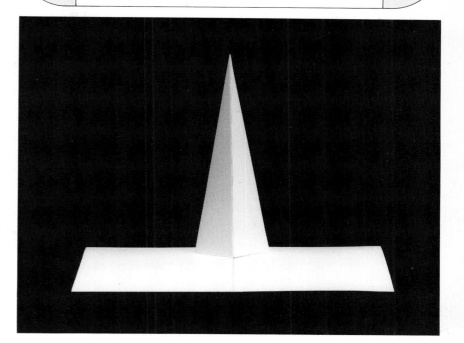

The Golden Gate, perhaps the best-known bridge in the world, is 9,184 feet in total length, with a span of 4,200 feet. It soars 216 feet above the surface of the water. For twenty-seven years, until the Verrazano-Narrows Bridge was built in New York, the Golden Gate Bridge was the longest suspension bridge in the world. The Verrazano-Narrows Bridge has a span of 4,260 feet and stands 228 feet above the water.

The engineer Othmar H. Ammann was born in Switzerland and was a master who planned six great bridges, beginning with the George Washington Bridge in New York (1931; span: 3,500 feet; height above the water: 212 feet) and culminating in the Verrazano-Narrows Bridge. Suspension bridges, though beautiful, are difficult to design. If there is a flaw in the design, a slight tremor may cause the bridge to sway and ripple violently. The continued stability of these bridges attests to Ammann's genius as an engineer.

There are now longer bridges all over the world, but the sweeping impression of the Golden Gate is second to none.

Please note that the base of the vertical cables should be a long valley fold; we were unable to include the fold line in the illustration.

Be extremely patient as you cut. Be sure to cut out the two big curves so that they have an easy feeling of stability. Cut out the space under the cables carefully and accurately. Be patient! Once you've cut out the design, the remaining paper will be extremely narrow and fragile, so take care as you fold.

1933–37

Joseph B. Strauss (1870–1938), chief engineer
Othmar H. Ammann (1879–1965)
Leon S. Moisseiff (1876–1943)
Charles Derleth, Jr., consultant

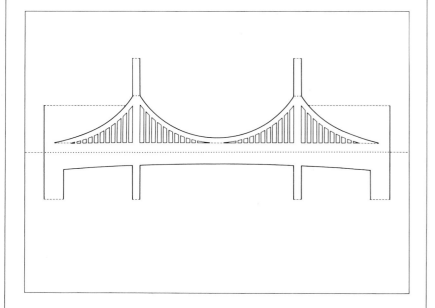

The skyline of San Francisco changed suddenly in 1976 with the appearance of this 48-floor, 853-foot tower. At the time, this brash, attention-grabbing building was criticized by many as ruining the elegant skyline of San Francisco, but the president of the company at the time was quite content with its advertising potential. Now the TransAmerica Pyramid sets San Francisco apart from other cities.

The pyramid shape is not merely a publicity device. Montgomery Street is the heart of San Francisco's financial district, and the tall, boxy skyscrapers lining the street form a sort of wind tunnel known to San Franciscans as The Canyon. The TransAmerica Pyramid, near the end of this line of buildings, lets in needed sunlight and warmth.

When the Eiffel Tower was first built, it was met with harsh criticism, especially from cultural figures such as Émile Zola. They said that the only way to avoid seeing this ugly tower was to ascend it. But before they knew it, the tower had transformed itself into a symbol of Paris, inseparable from the city. This type of rapid reversal of critical reception occurs more and more frequently as the twentieth century draws to a close.

See the step-by-step instructions on page 23. This type of design, which I've called the "perfect 180-degree" type, requires several sheets of paper joined together with durable, lightweight paper like Japanese washi; with softer paper, the folds can move very freely. Then, when the card is opened 180 degrees, the building pops out to form a sharp figure.

The design is somewhat complicated, and gluing it together is rather bothersome, but it will give you extra joy when you see it completed.

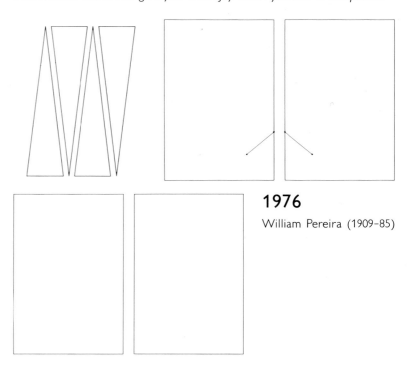

1976

William Pereira (1909–85)

<table>
<tr><td>

24   **SAN FRANCISCO**   Level B

San Francisco Skyline

</td><td>

25   **LOS ANGELES**   Level C

Hollywood Sign

</td></tr>
</table>

View from the Golden Gate Bridge

In the eighteenth century, this area was colonized by Franciscan monks from Spain, who named the city after St. Francis. In the nineteenth century, people flooded into the city during the California gold rush, and it developed even further when in 1869 it became the terminus of the transcontinental railroad.

The city was almost totally destroyed in the 1906 earthquake, but its reconstruction left the original city plan intact. In the middle of all the skyscrapers, the most striking building is the TransAmerica Pyramid (no. 23). The square building on the right side of the design is the Bank of America Building (1968), a representative work by Skidmore, Owings, and Merrill, one of the largest architectural firms in the world.

At the left side of the card is the Bay Bridge, which connects San Francisco to Oakland and the rest of the East Bay. The bridge was built by the same engineer who designed the Golden Gate.

This is a very complicated design, but by now, after all this experience, you know the fundamentals, and this is a design where you can pass off some rough work on the details as style. This may be because San Francisco itself is a forgiving and liberal city. Cut carefully, paying special attention to the cables of the bridge. If you make half-cuts on the back of card for the long valley folds, the folding will be easier and cleaner. After folding the center valley fold, proceed with the lower buildings in the front and work your way up to the taller buildings.

With no identifiable center and spreading out in all directions, Los Angeles symbolizes the western United States. Although the city is full of unique and interesting architecture, nothing embodies it as well as this sign, its letters strung out on the Hollywood Hills, which anyone — even people who have never visited the United States — can recognize immediately.

The sign was built in 1923 by a real-estate developer and originally read "Hollywoodland," advertising a real-estate development below Mount Lee, where the sign stands. The letters are 50 feet high and are made of sheet metal painted white and outlined by lightbulbs. In 1946 the sign was given to the city of Los Angeles and the *-land* was taken down. The sign fell into a state of disrepair, but was restored in 1978 with contributions from actors and actresses in the movie industry.

Cut out the insides of the O's and D first, and then cut from small to large as usual. When folding, be sure to fold all of the letters at once instead of doing one at a time. This simple design can be applied to any word or message. Simply place a piece of tracing paper over the Hollywood sign pattern and sketch in the letters of your message using the letters of the sign as guides. Trace the center valley fold and the vertical bars connecting each letter to the back of the card, and then transfer your pattern onto card stock using Method 2 (page 25). If you would like to make a card with different types of letters, it will be easier if you draw the letters so that the bottom of the center bar of a letter H falls exactly on the center valley fold.

1923

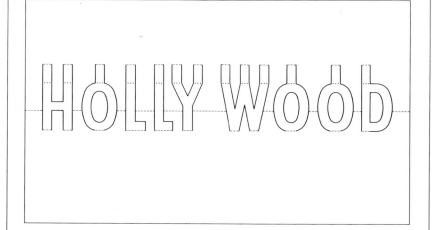

General Information

TOOLS AND MATERIALS

1. RULERS
You should have two rulers, one of clear plastic and another of metal.

2. STYLUS
The stylus was first invented to mark stencil paper. It resembles a pencil with a metal point instead of a lead. It will be used here to score fold lines and make holes. If a stylus is unobtainable, use a compass or divider to punch holes, and an inkless ballpoint pen or a paper knife to score lines.

3. TWEEZERS
You should choose a pair of tweezers with sharp, pointed ends for grasping small areas, making slight corrections, and other detailed work.

4. SNAP-OFF CUTTER
This or any type of small craft-knife with a sharp edge and a pointed tip will work. You should use one you feel comfortable with.

5. UNDERLAY
The underlay may be either thick plastic or cardboard. It serves not only to protect your desk or table but, more importantly, to make the cutting easier.

6. GLUE (for nos. 16 and 23 only)
Graphic paste or non-water-based glue.

PERFECT 180–DEGREE CARD ONLY (For no. 23)

7. White *washi* (Japanese handmade paper) or any strong, lightweight white paper.

8. White cotton thread.

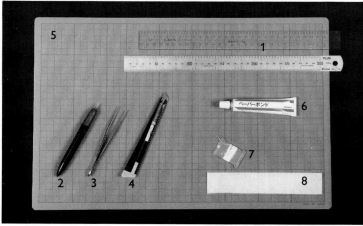

Tools

LEVEL OF DIFFICULTY
There are three levels of difficulty, "A" being the most advanced. For those readers desiring to start from the easier projects and work their way up to the hardest, projects are grouped here according to level:

A——10 · 18 · 20 · 23

B——1 · 2 · 4 · 6 · 7 · 8 · 13 · 14 · 15 · 17 · 19 · 21 · 22 · 24

C——3 · 5 · 9 · 11 · 12 · 16 · 25

METHOD 1
Using the Original Pattern

■ 90–DEGREE POP-UP PROJECTS (Nos. 1–22, 24–25)

These basic origami architecture projects each involve making a pop-up card from one sheet of paper folded to 90 degrees. Before starting, it is advisable to make a photocopy of the pattern. Not only will this allow you to make additional models at a later date by following Method 2, but the copy will be a useful reference for checking the convex and concave lines as you work. If you are using the original patterns, you should be advised that the printed lines, though light, will show. The AT&T Building (no. 3) is the example used below.

1. Tear out the pattern page.

2. Make a photocopy for future use.

3. Place the pattern face-up on the underlay and, using the metal ruler, trim away excess paper around the borderlines with the cutter.

4. Score the valley folds (concave), which are indicated thus: - - -. To do this, align the ruler with the line to be scored and press firmly with the stylus, following the ruler's edge.
   When there are many small valley folds, turn the paper over and half-cut the lines from the back (*see next step*). This makes the eventual folding much easier. *Do not half-cut the two central valley folds.* These two folds should be as strong as possible in order for the card to stand at a 90-degree angle.

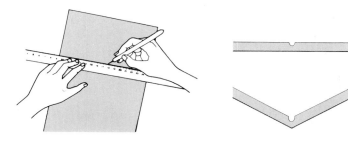

step 4   Score valley folds.

5. Prepare the mountain folds (convex), which are marked thus: · · · · · · ·. To do this, align the metal ruler with the convex line and draw the cutter blade lightly across the paper, cutting no deeper than halfway through. This half-cut will make it easier to fold, and the angle will be sharper and cleaner. Be very careful not to cut too deeply. If you do inadvertently cut through the paper, be sure to repair the cut before folding the card (*see Repairs*).

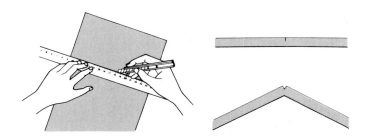

step 5   Half-cut mountain folds.

6. Cut the remaining lines. Use a metal ruler for the straight lines, but cut the curved lines freehand. When cutting along curved lines, such as the entrance of a building, it helps if you move the knife *and* the card, pulling them in opposite directions. A circle cutter is useful for large circles (no. 8), and a hole puncher or leather-craft punch is helpful for cutting small circles (no. 9). To make clean, precise cuts, you should do the following:

- Make sure you press down firmly with the ruler and pass the blade gently over the line two or three times, cutting completely through on the final pass.
- Cut at a right angle to the paper.
- Cut the shorter lines and areas clustered with many lines first, then cut the longer lines.
- When cutting an acute angle, cut toward the tip to get a sharp point (see *illustration 6a*).
- When cutting a corner, press the blade strongly from the tip (see *illustration 6b*).

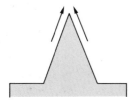
step 6a   For acute angles.

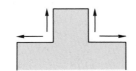
step 6b   To cut corners.

7. When the fold lines and cutting lines have been readied, the real origami begins. With the folding process, unlike the cutting process, you start with the major lines.

Before you begin pushing out the structure, check that you have cut the lines perfectly according to the pattern. To fold, lift the paper in both hands with the front side facing you and, from the back, start pushing out the mountain folds. The building will begin to emerge.

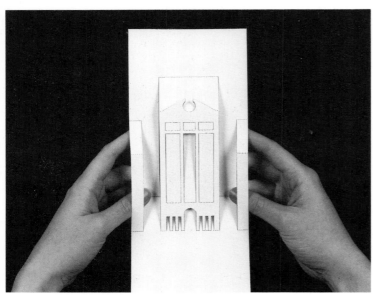
step 7a   Push out the structure. . . .

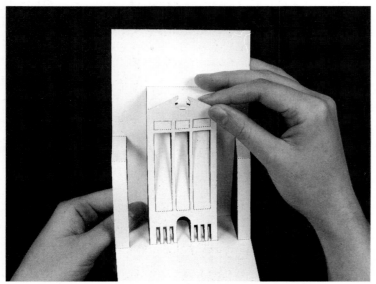
step 7b   Fold major lines (mountain folds) as you go.

Some parts may not push easily, probably because the cutting has been insufficient. If this occurs, stop and check the lines. *The folding/ pressing out should never be done quickly. Fold slowly, frequently referring to the photograph of the completed card.*

Occasionally, while pushing the form out, some fold lines may be too stiff and resist your attempts to fold them. For mountain folds, return the paper to its flat state and half-cut the problematic lines a little more deeply. On occasion some flat areas may show signs of creasing. When this happens, avoid putting any pressure on that area.

For valley folds: Since each fold is dependent for its shape and strength on every other part of the structure, lightly press all the fold lines again, one by one, especially the center valley fold lines, then try the troublesome fold once more. If necessary, use the tweezers and the tip of the stylus.

8. To finish, continue to fold carefully until the two halves of the paper can be folded together. Make sure that all lines have been folded, then press the paper down firmly along the center line, completing the card. Press down hard on the structure inside. Open the card to 90 degrees.

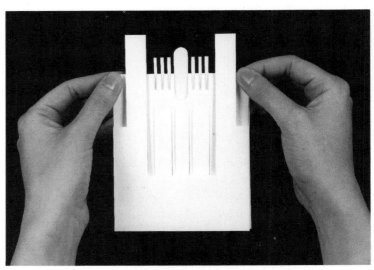
step 8   Fold in half and press the center line.

Completed card.

■ 180–DEGREE POP-UP PROJECT (No. 23)

This type of origami architecture project creates pop-up shapes that are held together by thread and durable lightweight paper. Because the card stock itself is never folded, the shapes can be more complex than the ordinary 90-degree projects (as well as the simpler 180-degree projects we introduced in our last book, *White Christmas*), and the card can be opened and closed repeatedly with ease. Also, it can be displayed on a shelf or other flat surface without supports. The TransAmerica Pyramid has such a simple structure that it is an excellent way to begin working on this type of origami architecture. In the future, perhaps we will write another book entirely made up of "perfect 180-degree" designs.

1. Tear out the pattern page.

2. Make a photocopy for future use.

3. Place the pattern face-up on the underlay and, using a metal ruler, carefully cut out the four small triangles. These will become the pyramid itself. Next, cut out the four squares. The two squares with lines printed on them will become the inside surface of the card, and the two blank squares will become the outside surface of the card.

step 3   Cut out pattern.

4. Place the four triangles together, face-down, so that the long sides match up. Be sure that the sides of the triangles are exactly the same length. If they are not, the completed pyramid will lean to one side.

5. Cut out 18 small ¼-inch-square pieces of white *washi* (Japanese handmade paper) or a similar thin, durable lightweight paper. Put a quantity of glue on a sheet of paper or in a dish and, picking up the squares with tweezers, dab each in the glue and paste to the sides of the triangles, as shown. (For purposes of illustration, the *washi* in the photograph is darker than standard *washi*.)

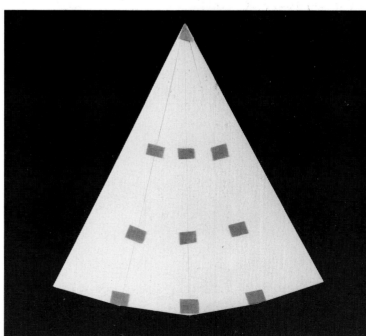

step 5   Join triangles with paper and glue.

6. Place 5-inch pieces of thread on top of the three squares you've already pasted on the bases of the triangles, and then paste new squares on top of the thread, as shown. These threads (colored black for this photograph) will be the only connection between the pyramid and the card, so paste carefully. The two layers of *washi* will help keep the threads in place.

step 6   Attach threads.

7. Form the pyramid by bringing the two outer edges of the triangles together. Make sure that the pyramid will stand straight without wobbling. Open up the pyramid again, paste three more squares of *washi* along one of the outer edges so that half of each square is free, and form the pyramid again, attaching the free halves of the *washi* squares to the opposite edge before the glue dries. Set the remaining three pieces of *washi* aside.

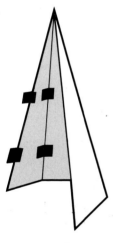

step 7a   Bring two outer edges together and glue.

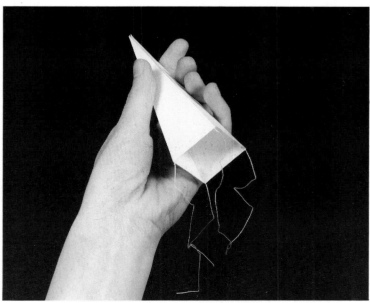

step 7b   Pyramid should look like this.

8. Cut a 6″ × ½″ strip of *washi*. Place the two base squares with lines on them next to each other so that the lines make a "V". Turn the base squares face-down with the "V" intact, and paste the *washi* along the point where the squares meet, as shown. While the glue is still wet, bring the two sides together and hold them in position until the glue dries. Then open the card again, making sure that there is a slight gap between the edges of the card (*see illustration 8b*). Trim off the excess *washi* at top and bottom.

step 8a   Glue two sides of card together with a long strip of paper.

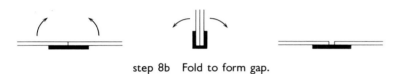

step 8b   Fold to form gap.

9. Turn the card face-up so that the "V" is inverted. Place the pyramid so that two of its sides are aligned with the "V" to make sure that the corners meet the dots. Using the stylus, make one hole in the *washi* between the two top dots, and then make holes in each of the two bottom dots. With the tweezers (or a needle), push the three threads through the three holes, as shown. Note that the corner of the pyramid without thread is closest to you.

step 9a   Turn card over and punch three holes.

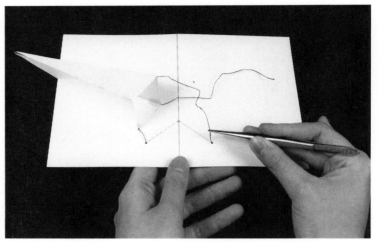

step 9b   Insert threads.

10. Pull the threads through so that they are taut, and temporarily attach each to the back of the base paper with cellophane tape. Open and close the card several times to make sure the pyramid stands up straight, adjusting the threads if necessary. Then paste the remaining three pieces of *washi* over the three holes on the back of the paper in order to fix the threads in place. Make a line of glue along the thread, and then remove the tape and trim off the excess thread. Finally, paste the blank squares to the back of the card, as shown.

step 10a   Secure threads firmly with *washi*.

step 10b   Paste remaining two squares over threads to cover.

Opening card

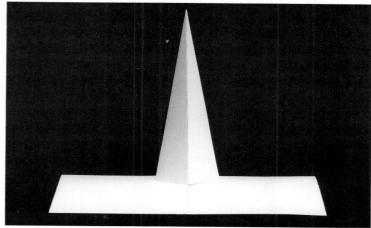

Completed card

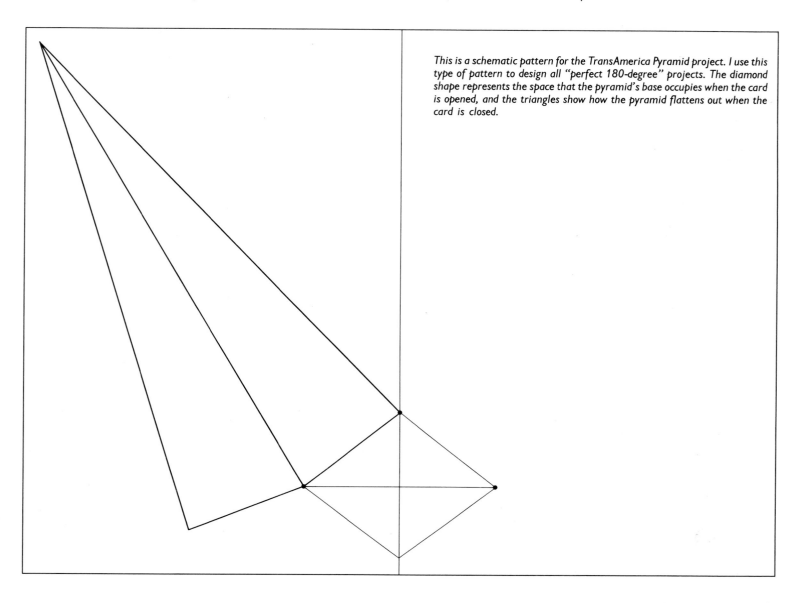

This is a schematic pattern for the TransAmerica Pyramid project. I use this type of pattern to design all "perfect 180-degree" projects. The diamond shape represents the space that the pyramid's base occupies when the card is opened, and the triangles show how the pyramid flattens out when the card is closed.

METHOD 2
Tracing the Pattern

You should use stiff (100-pound) card stock or stiff white paper for the 90-degree pop-ups. You can use slightly thinner paper than the pattern pages in the book for the 180-degree card (no. 23) since you will also be using stiff card stock for the base.

1. After selecting the paper, you must determine which way the fibers run. This is only necessary for the 90-degree pop-ups. When paper is manufactured, the fibers line up in the same direction; the strength of the fold lines will depend on the direction of the line relative to the fibers. To ascertain the direction of the fibers, cut a 2-inch square from the paper you wish to use. If you bend it with two fingers, you will realize very quickly that the paper bends more easily in one direction than in the other. The direction in which it bends most easily is the direction in which the fibers run. The central valley fold of the card should run perpendicular to the direction of the fibers to give the pop-up building strength.

step 1   Central valley fold.

step 1   Test the paper for direction of fibers.

2. Make a photocopy of the original.

3. Place the stiff paper on the underlay, and lay the copied pattern on top.

4. Using the tip of a stylus or compass, make small holes at every corner or junction where lines meet, starting with the six points around the border of the card. For curved lines, prick many points along the curve. When there are many complicated curves, use the stylus and press firmly along the curved line. Keeping the two sheets aligned, carefully hold them up to the light to verify that you have marked all the points.

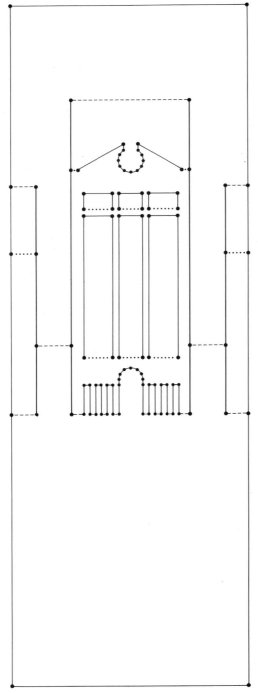

step 4　Make a hole at every corner.

5. The puncture marks will serve as your reference for cutting and building the origami. Referring to the original pattern as often as necessary, proceed according to Method 1 (beginning from step 4).

VARIATIONS

Miniature-size: Simply use a reduced photocopy to make the pattern for small-sized cards. When the scale is smaller, however, the cutting and folding require a much more delicate touch. The drastic reduction in size may also necessitate elimination of a few details. If you use any of the patterns on pages 9 to 20, you can make miniature-size cards easily according to Method 2.

If small-scale projects intrigue you, you might consider making three-dimensional name cards.

Poster-size: When making a particularly large example — say, for an exhibition — the pattern must be replotted. To do this, draw a ¼-inch-square grid over a copy of the original pattern in this book. Draw a larger grid on the larger sheet of paper and redraw the pattern, square by square.

As the size of the card increases, not only must the pattern be adjusted but the thickness of the paper must be increased proportionately.

When you have chosen appropriate paper, do not forget to check the direction of the fibers, as explained in the first step in Method 2.

Changing the card size: The cards in this book are of several sizes. It is possible to increase or decrease the size of the card itself (that is, the border around the origami) to fit a specific envelope or other requirement, but the change should not be too extreme. Either of these adjustments are easily made; however, when reducing the border, be careful not to trim too much, or the structure may stick out when the card is folded in two.

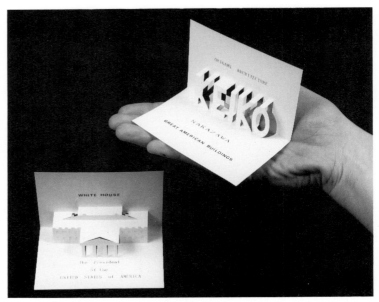

Pop-up name cards.

REPAIRS

When you have cut a fold line by mistake . . .
Washi (Japanese handmade paper) is highly recommended, but any strong, lightweight white paper can be used to make the repair. Cut the paper into very small pieces and glue it to the back of the card using a non-water-based glue. (Water-based glues cause stiff paper to swell.) This is detailed work, so the tweezers are of immense value.

When a thin strip of paper has weakened and shows signs of creasing . . .
Using a non-water-based glue, reinforce the weakened area by gluing a fragment of the same type of paper to the back. Make sure it doesn't show from the front.

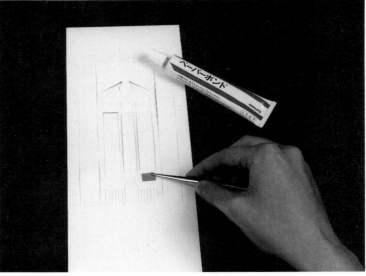

Glue paper to the back of the card.

END NOTE

American architecture, with its diverse national and cultural roots, has a depth and richness of scope that often seems diluted since the sites of its prime examples are scattered across the continent. In *American Homes* I explored this theme with reference to where people live and sleep. In this volume, I would like to look at characteristic buildings of state, culture, and the workplace.

While most of us know George Washington as a president and a general, few realize he was also a trained surveyor and an amateur architect with a keen sense of design. In 1752 he took over the family home, Mount Vernon, and went to work enlarging the mansion. In 1759 he added a full second story and in 1785 he added two-story extensions to both sides of the main building, and even erected a fourteen-foot-wide, two-story-high "piazza," or porch. The design of these additions went beyond the Georgian style in which Mount Vernon had originally been built, and I like to look on this as the birth of a new American style.

While in Philadelphia in 1787, Washington worked with a young French military engineer, Pierre Charles L'Enfant, to lay out a plan for a new capital city. L'Enfant completed the plan in 1791 and the capital of the United States was established on a square site thirteen miles up the Potomac River from Mount Vernon. Looking back through time from the 1990s, L'Enfant's plan seems to have been successful for two reasons (even though it was modified to some extent). First, his ideas for a capital city were based not on 13 colonies and 3 million inhabitants but on a larger vision of a republic "ultimately having 50 states and 500 million inhabitants." Second, L'Enfant had reached artistic maturity in Paris and Versailles, where he was strongly influenced by Baroque landscape architecture. L'Enfant's dream was to build the Paris of the New World. However, the people of late-eighteenth-century America thought his ideas too fantastic, and he was dismissed before even the first cornerstone was laid. L'Enfant's original plan was effectively lost until 1887, when its recovery revealed that a number of nineteenth-century buildings along Pennsylvania Avenue, around the White House, and on Capitol Hill had altered L'Enfant's original symmetries.

Whenever I take a stroll through the streets of Washington, I see magnificent buildings and marvelously appropriate street names like Independence and Constitution avenues that symbolize the spirit of America. The 545-foot-tall Washington Monument stands in the heart of the capital. To the north is the White House. Reflected in the waters of the tidal basin is the

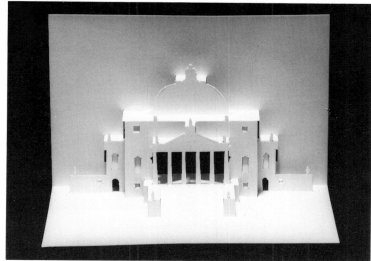

Palladio's pride: La Rotonda—the epitome of his style and an inspiration to Jefferson. Vicenza, Italy, 1566–67.

Jefferson Memorial and to the west is the Lincoln Memorial. As I walk along the mall, I see museums, the Capitol Building, the Supreme Court, and the Library of Congress, and I want to transform all of them into origami architecture.

Author of the Declaration of Independence (1776) and the third president (1801–1809), Thomas Jefferson (1743–1826) was also a talented architect who ranked with the professionals. He is known not only for his home Monticello (1770–1808) in Charlottesville, Virginia, but also for the Virginia state Capitol Building (1789–98) in Richmond and the campus of the University of Virginia (1817–26). These buildings were designed in the Palladian style, named after the Italian architect Andrea Palladio (1508–80). Thomas Jefferson can thus be said to have had a great influence on the neoclassical style in the United States.

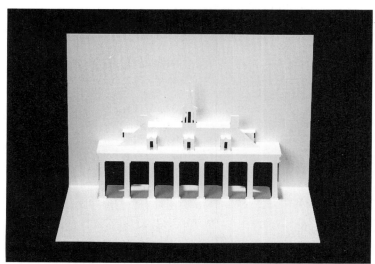

Mount Vernon: The first stirrings of an American architecture.

Another of New York's inimitable monuments: The CBS Building, 1960–64, by Eero Saarinen.

New York, New York.... After Washington, D.C., I find that New York is the most representative American city, with a history as interesting as its architecture. Manhattan comes from an Indian word meaning "a layer of rock," and before the Dutch purchased it for 60 guilders' worth of trinkets (about $24) in 1626, it belonged to the Indians. The Dutch called it New Amsterdam, and after bloody clashes with the Indians in 1643 and 1655, they built a fort to protect the city in 1660. The fort, however, couldn't keep the British out, and in 1664, when the land was given to the Duke of York, the younger brother of King Charles II, New Amsterdam became New York.

New York extended northward and eventually covered all of Manhattan with a grid of streets and avenues, turning it into a true city. In 1870 the world's first elevator was installed in a six-story New York building, making tall buildings both practical and possible. But New York was not alone in its race for the sky. The Great Chicago Fire in 1871 meant that the first buildings with iron frames were built outside of New York, and from the ashes of the fire the Chicago school of early modern architecture was born.

Whereas Washington, D.C., has the character of a true "city of monuments," New York (notwithstanding its own great monument, the Statue of Liberty) has more the character of a "city of the monumental"; Manhattan's dense skyline of high-rise structures gives New York a super-human scale which is sometimes awe-inspiring, sometimes simply awful, but always memorable.

Chicago has perhaps more than its share of monumental buildings, but west of the Atlantic seaboard few true monuments are to be found — with the notable exception of the elegant Gateway Arch in St. Louis, a grand formal gesture to the historic idea of "the West" when America was still young and growing.

Hundreds of miles farther westward stands another tall structure, one which straddles the fence between being a monument and being simply monumental; I am referring to San Francisco's TransAmerica Building — better known as the TransAmerica Pyramid, with a somewhat less grand and much less formal gesture to historic Egypt. A distinctive but frankly jarring element in San Francisco's otherwise conservative skyline, it is hard to say whether the TransAmerica Building's attention-grabbing presence is due more to its form or its great height.

But height is not everything. I believe that in the future we will have to take more care with the fragile environment of our spaceship Earth. Instead of aiming at the sky with taller and taller buildings, we should perhaps pay more attention to what is happening on the ground. Human scale and the quality of the spaces which people experience must not be forgotten by future high-rise developers. At any rate, nearly half the book is filled with skyscrapers so that you can build buildings with unlimited stories and aim at the sky in this harmless way.

Masahiro Chatani

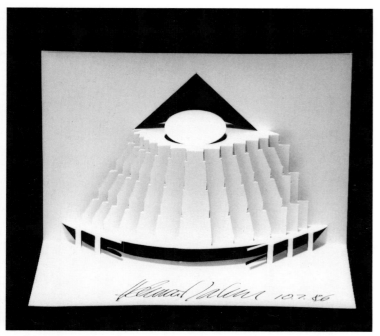

A jewel in Chicago's crown: The State of Illinois Center, 1985, by H. Jahn.

Bibliography

Morgan, Ann Lee, and Naylor, Colin, *Contemporary Architects*, St. James Press, 1987.

Smith, George Everard Kidder, *The Architecture of the United States*, vols. 1–3, New York, Anchor Books/Doubleday, 1981.

Willensky, Elliot, and White, Norval, *AIA Guide to New York City*, New York, Harcourt Brace Jovanovich, 1988.

Acknowledgments

We would like to thank Michiko Uchiyama, our editor, for her sterling effort in planning this project, and Laura Jones for her valuable editorial help. We would also like to express our gratitude to Barry Lancet for his advice and for suggesting we try our hand at depicting some of America's most famous skylines. We are indebted to Neil Warren, a practicing architect working in Tokyo who helped bridge the language barrier in regard to some of the more technical information, and to Paul Hulbert for his last-minute assistance.

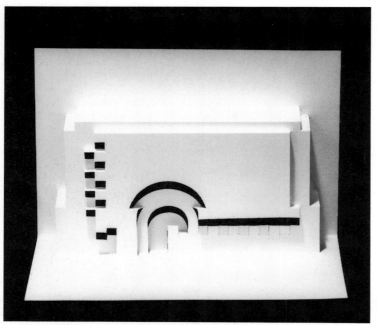

A San Francisco gem: Morris Shop, 1948, by Frank Lloyd Wright.

· · · · · mountain fold
- - - - valley fold
——— cutting line

· · · · · mountain fold
- - - - valley fold
——— cutting line

5 NEW YORK

see page 11

Flatiron Building

Level C

····· mountain fold
----- valley fold
—— cutting line

6 NEW YORK

see page 11

Statue of Liberty

Level B

····· mountain fold
----- valley fold
—— cutting line

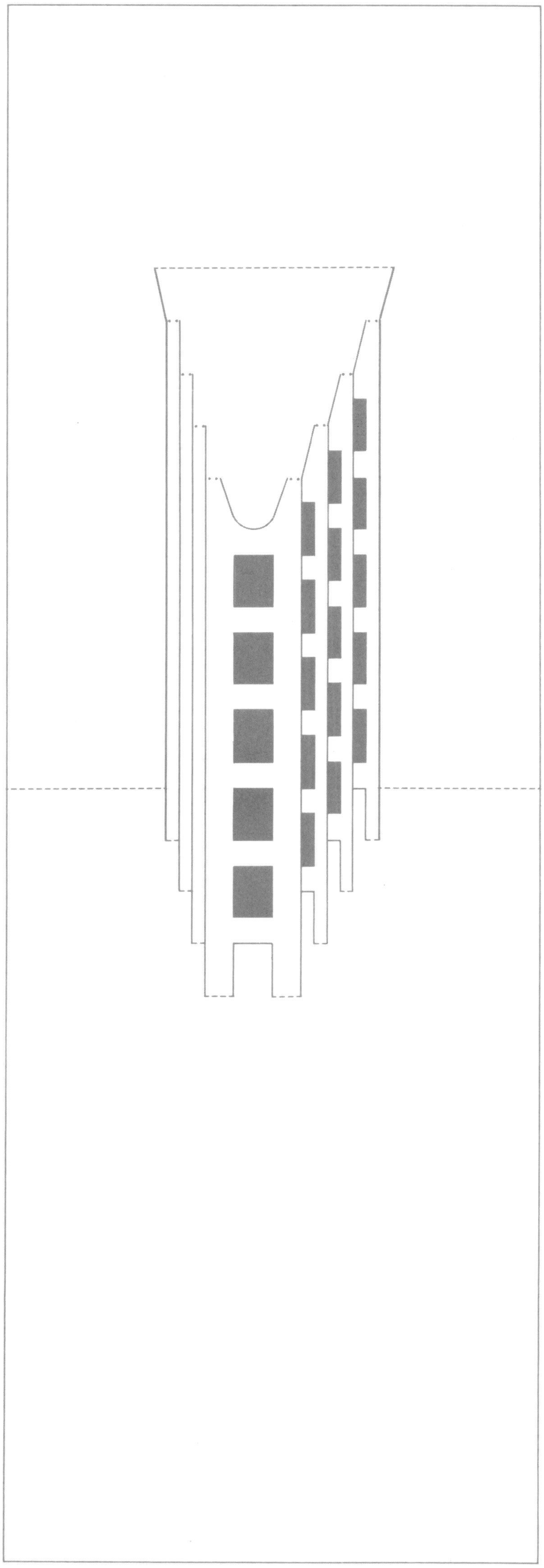

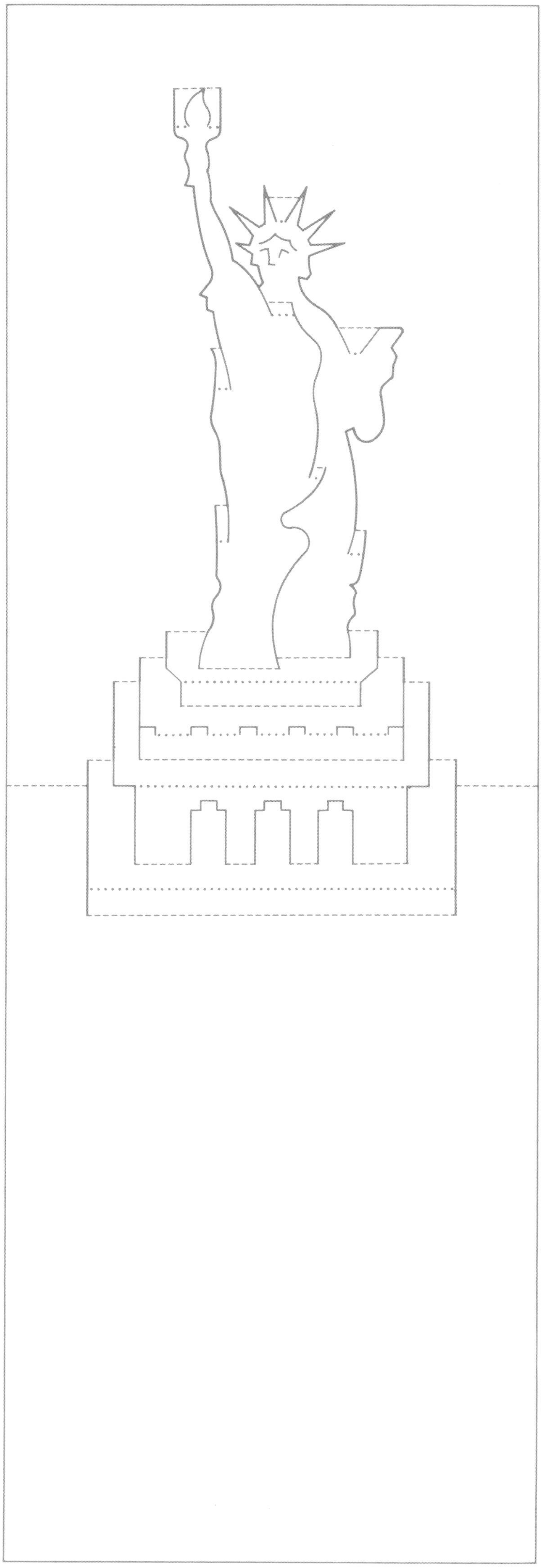

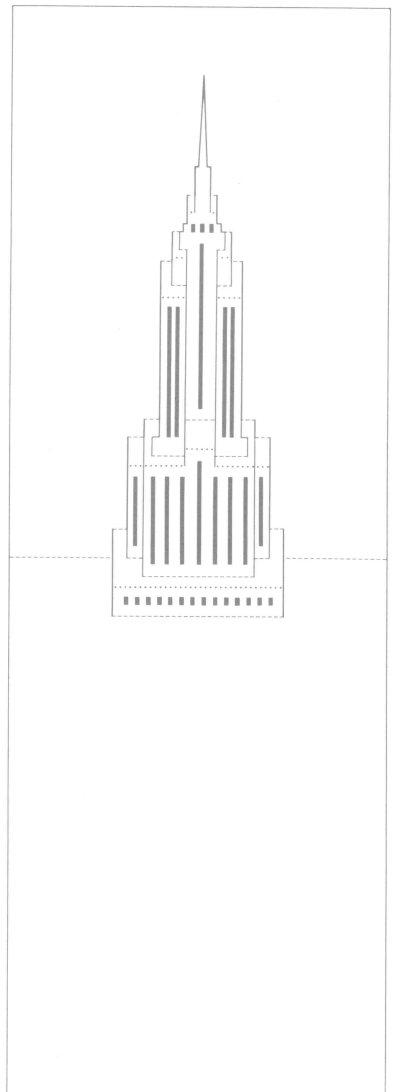

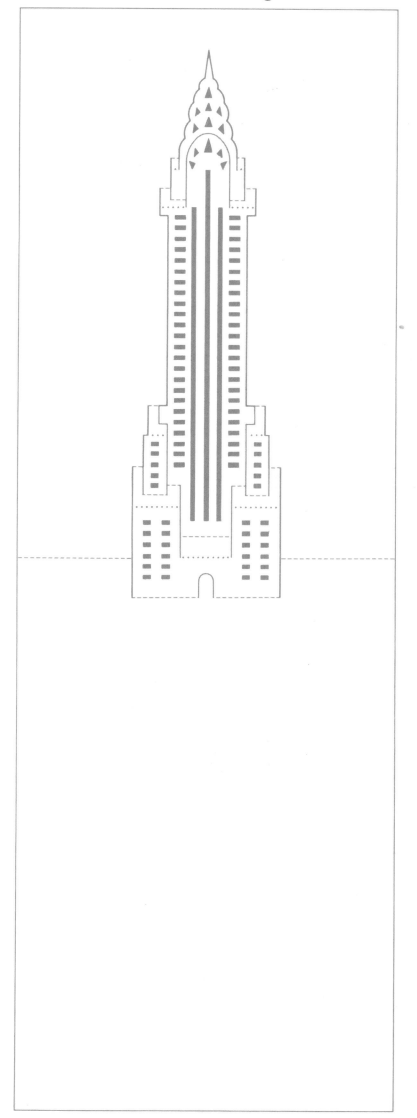

· · · · · mountain fold
- - - - valley fold
—— cutting line

· · · · · mountain fold
- - - - valley fold
—— cutting line

3 | AT&T Building

see page 10

Level C

4 | Trump Tower

see page 10

Level B

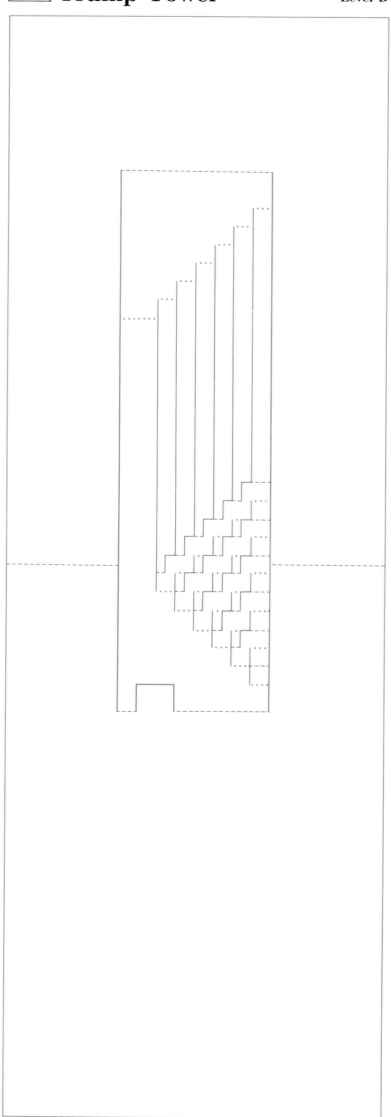

·····mountain fold
- - - - -valley fold
——— cutting line

·····mountain fold
- - - - -valley fold
——— cutting line

· · · · · mountain fold
- - - - - valley fold
——— cutting line

Guggenheim Museum

Level B

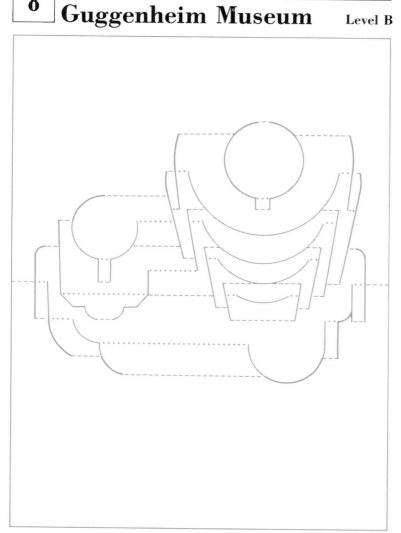

····· mountain fold
----- valley fold
——— cutting line

Museum of Modern Art

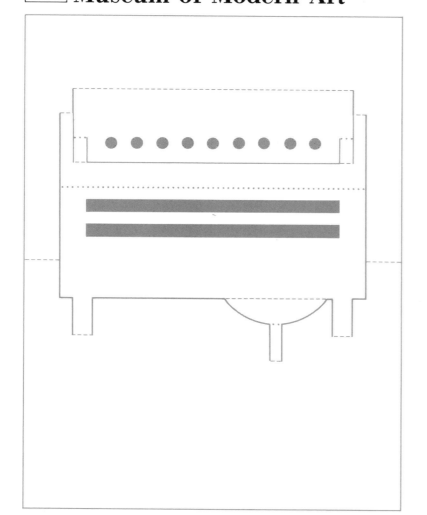

····· mountain fold
----- valley fold
——— cutting line

Capitol Building

Level A

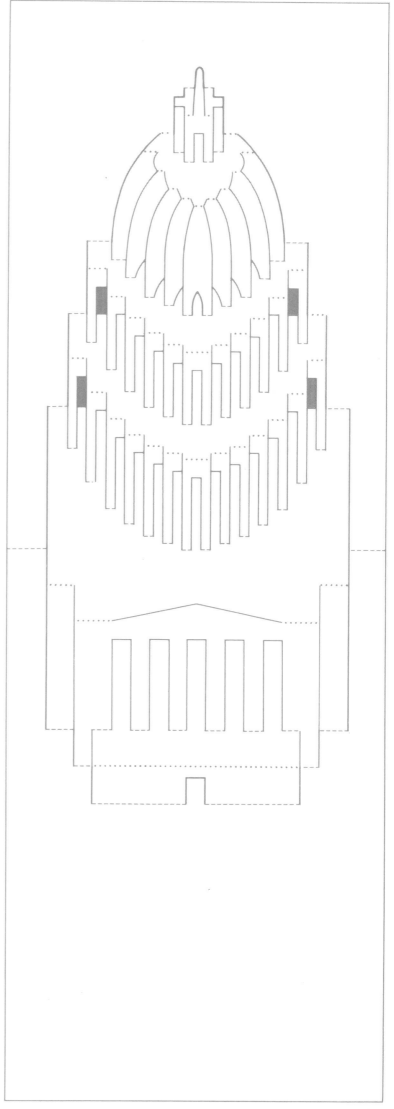

····· mountain fold
----- valley fold
——— cutting line

.....mountain fold
- - - - valley fold
——— cutting line

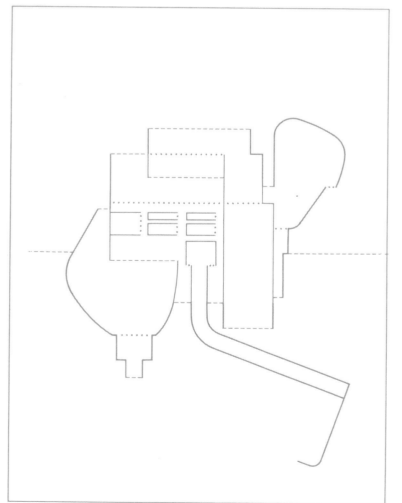

.....mountain fold
- - - - valley fold
——— cutting line

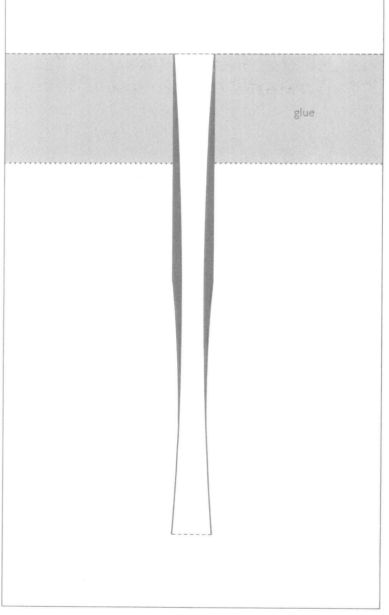

glue

.....mountain fold
- - - - valley fold
——— cutting line

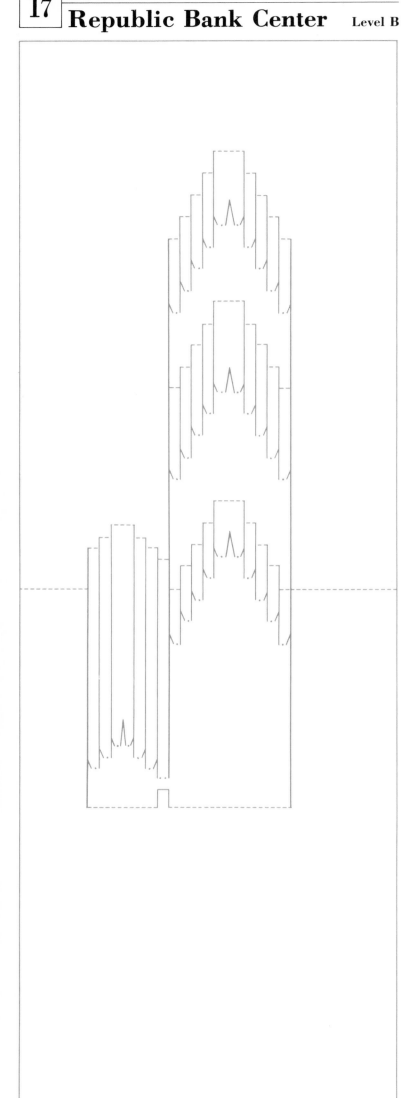

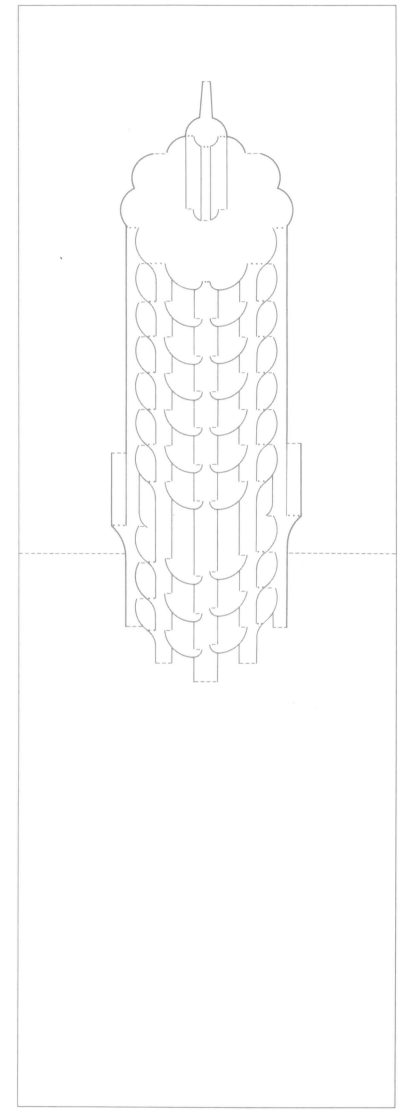

· · · · · mountain fold
- - - - - valley fold
——— cutting line

· · · · · mountain fold
- - - - - valley fold
——— cutting line

Crown Hall (Illinois Institute of Technology)

mountain fold
valley fold
cutting line

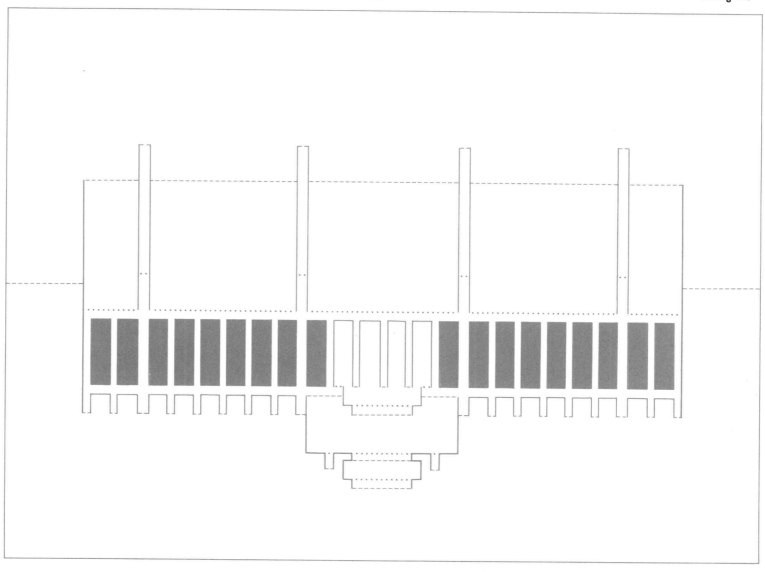

Johnson Wax Buildings

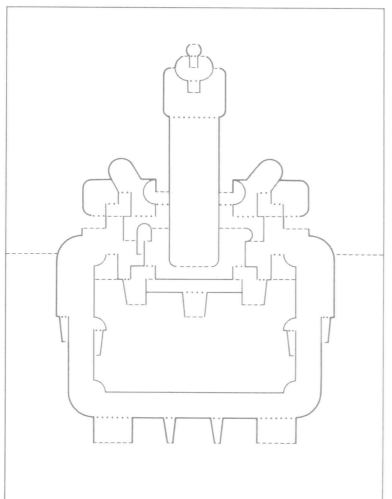

mountain fold
valley fold
cutting line

Hyatt Regency Hotel   Level B

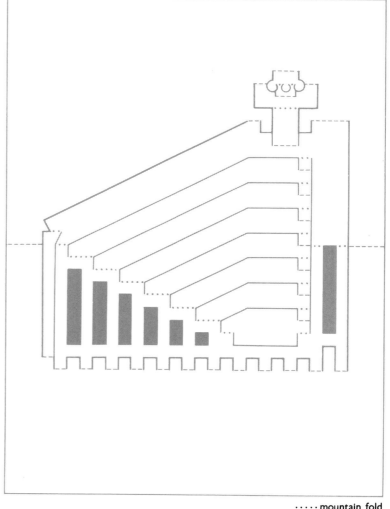

mountain fold
valley fold
cutting line